SACRED THREADS

Liturgical Exhibit

Floris United Methodist Church invited artists to submit works to be displayed in our chapel and sanctuary during the 2015 Sacred Threads exhibit. It is our hope that as you view the art in these sacred spaces God will bless you. If you would like to sit or pray quietly in these spaces please know you are welcome.

To learn more about Floris United Methodist Church, visit: www.florisumc.org

Sacred Threads is grateful to the generosity and hospitality of the Floris United Methodist Church family and staff.

Sacred Threads is known for our biennial exhibition of quilts exploring themes of spirituality, joy, grief, healing, inspiration, and peace/brotherhood.

Visit us online: www.sacredthreadsquilts.com

For more information about Sacred Threads, contact Lisa Ellis at lisa@ellisquilts.com.

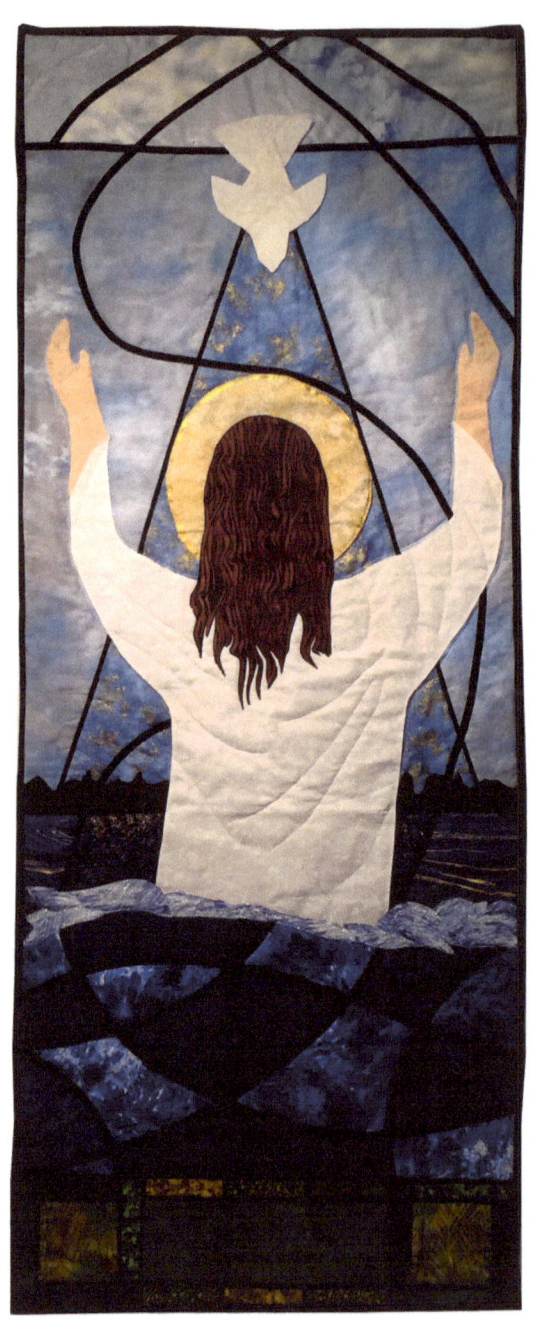

Lisa Arthaud

Warrenton, VA, USA

This Is My Beloved
24" x 60"

"Christ Our Lord Has Risen!"

"Our Lord Has Risen Indeed!"

"Alleluia!"

Easter Church Service has always been my favorite. This year, upon hearing the words, "Our Lord Has Risen", I had an epiphany. As the Gospel of Mark begins with the Baptism of Jesus, I envisioned Christ surging upwards through the water, rejoicing with the Holy Spirit. I also envisioned Jesus joyfully rising forth with his glorious ascension into heaven.

From Baptism to our death, we are called to "rise up" and meet each day as a gift. A day to seek, serve, create, and rejoice.

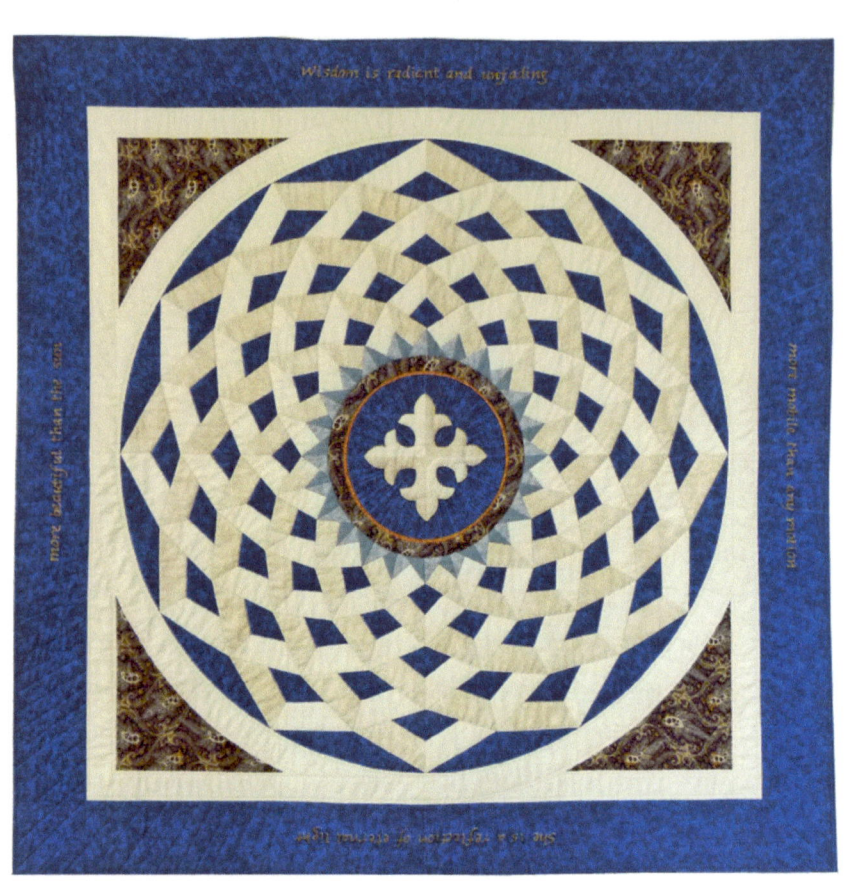

Kay Benedict
Saint Albans, VT, USA

The Wisdom Quilt
53.5" x 53.5"

The imagery in the "Book of Wisdom" (1st century BC) is beautiful and powerful. The personification of Wisdom is said to be a reflection of God and a view of the Messiah to come.

I began this quilt from Norah McMeeking's pattern simply as an exercise in paper piecing, but I was inspired to transform the design into an expression of the imagery in these verses. The words in the border are taken from the "Book of Wisdom".

"Wisdom is radiant and unfading,
more mobile than any motion.
She is a reflection of eternal light,
more beautiful than the sun."

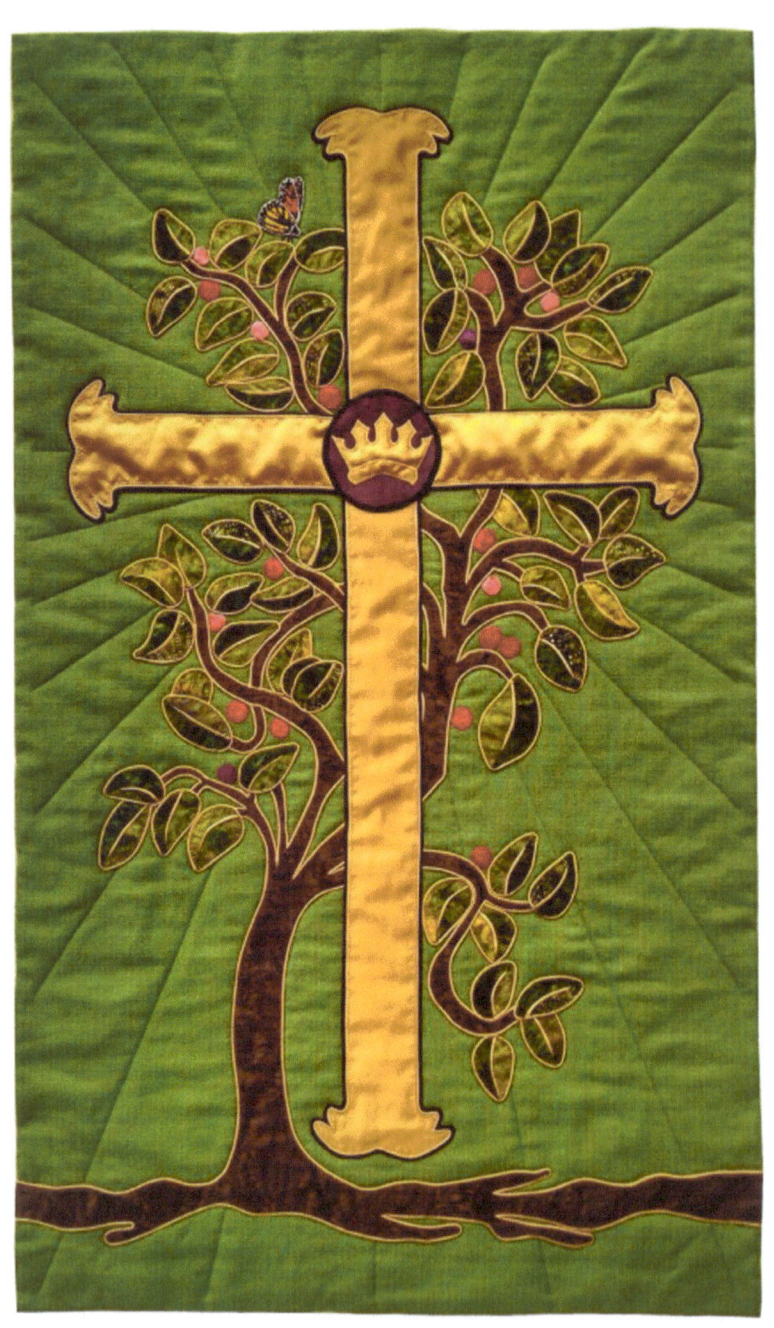

Sarah Brandt
China Grove, NC, USA

Tree of Life
33" x 56"

The banner is filled with symbolism from scripture. Jesus' death and resurrection is depicted by the cross and crown. The tree of life reminds us of Revelations 22: 2 and stands as an invitation to the world to return to Christ. "The leaves of the tree will be used for the healing of the nations." In a world that desperately needs the healing touch of our Savior, we also remember 2 Chronicles 7:14" . . . that he will hear us from heaven, forgive our sins, and heal the land". The fruit calls us to remember the fruits of the Spirit.

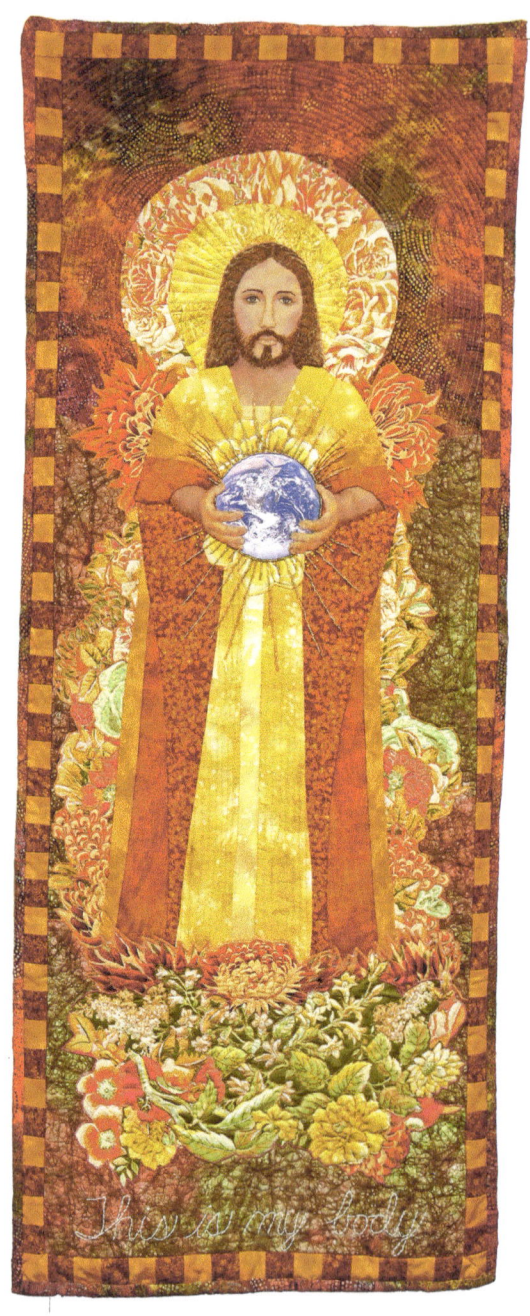

Carol Bridges
Nashville, IN, USA

This is My Body
24" x 60"

I see Jesus offering us the planet Earth and telling us that this is His Body. Instead of merely holding up bread as His offering, He shows us that everything which brings us that bread is also His body. All life is connected. All life is a gift. All life is sacred. Treating everything as God's body is an earth-regenerating point-of-view so greatly needed at this time.

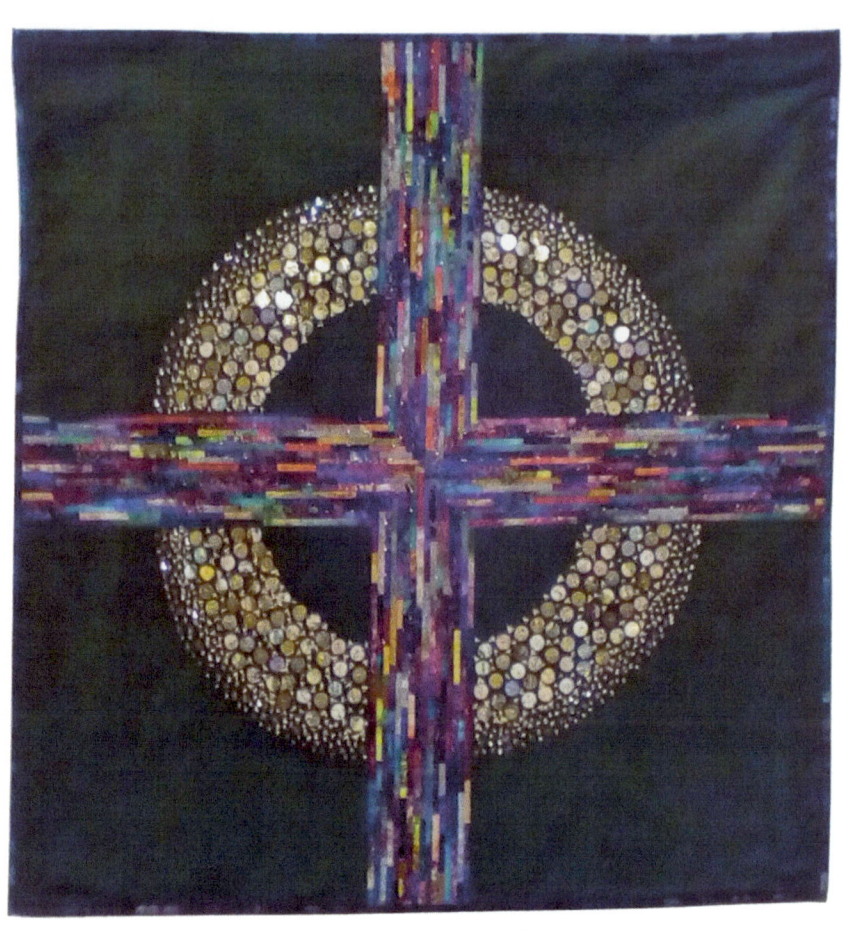

Laura Broderick
Rockville, MD, USA

Joyful
36" x 36"

My first mosaic cross was completed more than 20 years ago to challenge myself to quilt in small patchwork with more detail work. The search for colors and materials is where I begin an inspiration, but the transformation of the idea to a creation is a process of joy, patience and challenge. I love and enjoy the detail required to make something one of a kind.

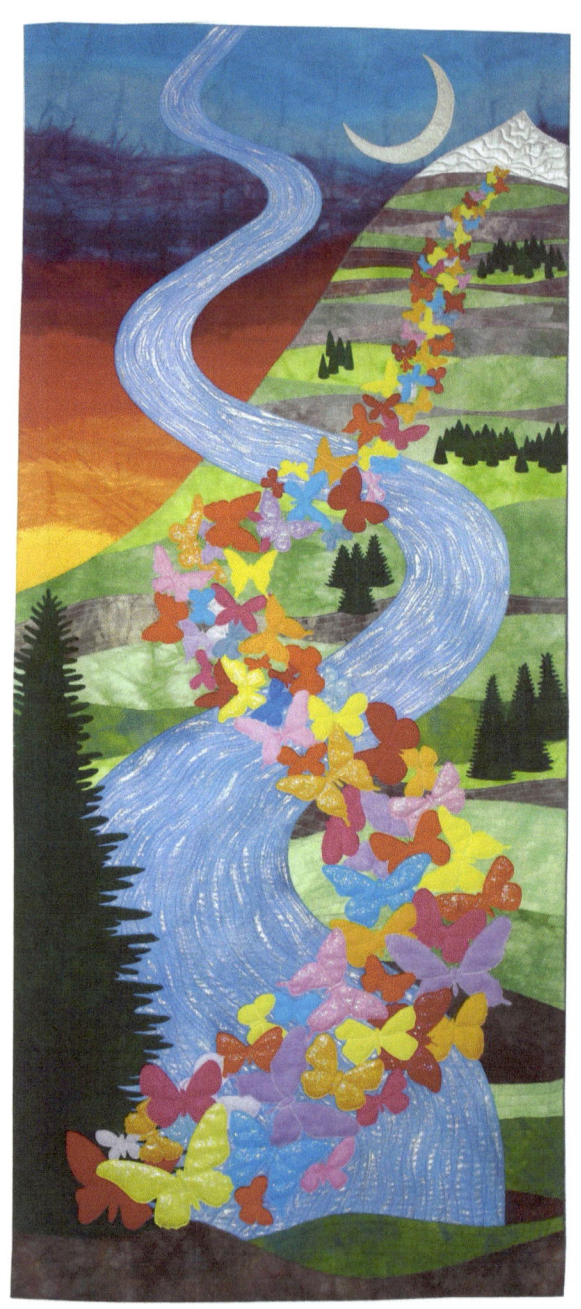

Karen Brown
Westminster, MD, USA

Climbing The Mountain
26" x 62"

Faith traditions speak of the mountaintop experience as part of the spiritual journey. It could be the result of a long, hard struggle searching for answers. It could come after a period of discernment. It could appear as you open a new door after a transition. But unlike climbing a physical mountain, the spiritual mountaintop experience cannot be planned – it is through grace that we are gifted with it. By opening, listening, and traveling on our spiritual path, we put faith into action and put our souls on the mountain. This quilted journey is also fed by the river of life touching and crossing the path of butterflies.

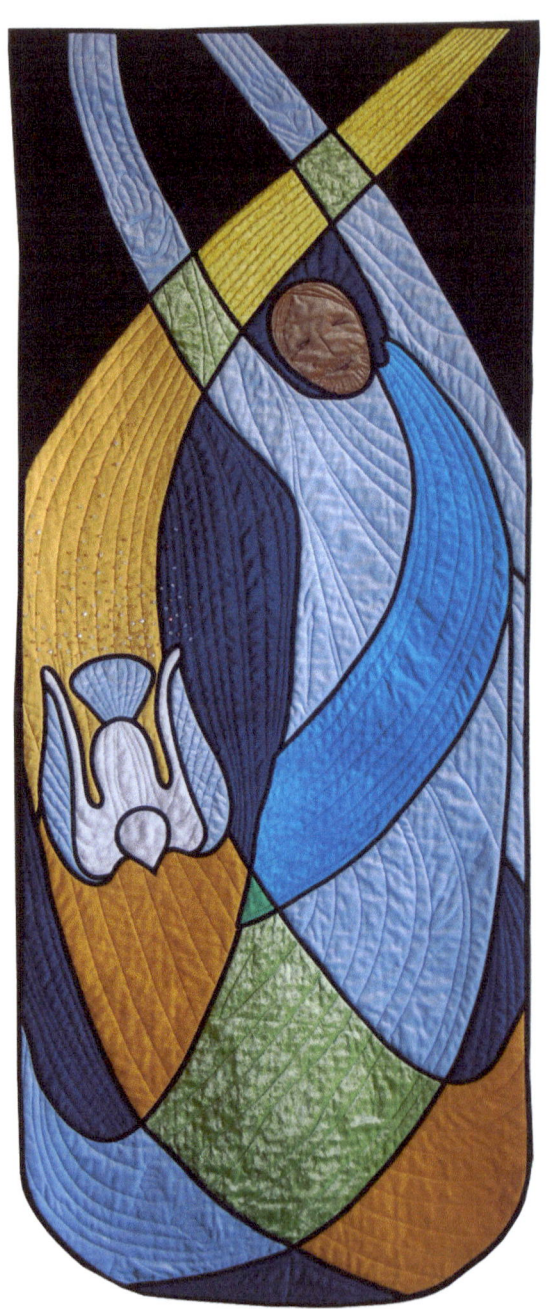

M. Bunte
West Lafayette, IN, USA

Sending/Ascending
25" x 61"

At the beginning of the book of Acts, the risen Lord returns to be with His Father. His apostles may have felt that they were being abandoned by their leader. They surely did not want to say goodbye to Him. But before leaving, He promises that the world will not be left alone, untended. God's spirit, also called the Comforter, soon descends to provide spiritual warmth and protection for them. The apostles become courageous messengers of God's love and compassion through His Spirit, a message that continues even now. What quilter would not understand the feelings of security associated with the word "comforter"?

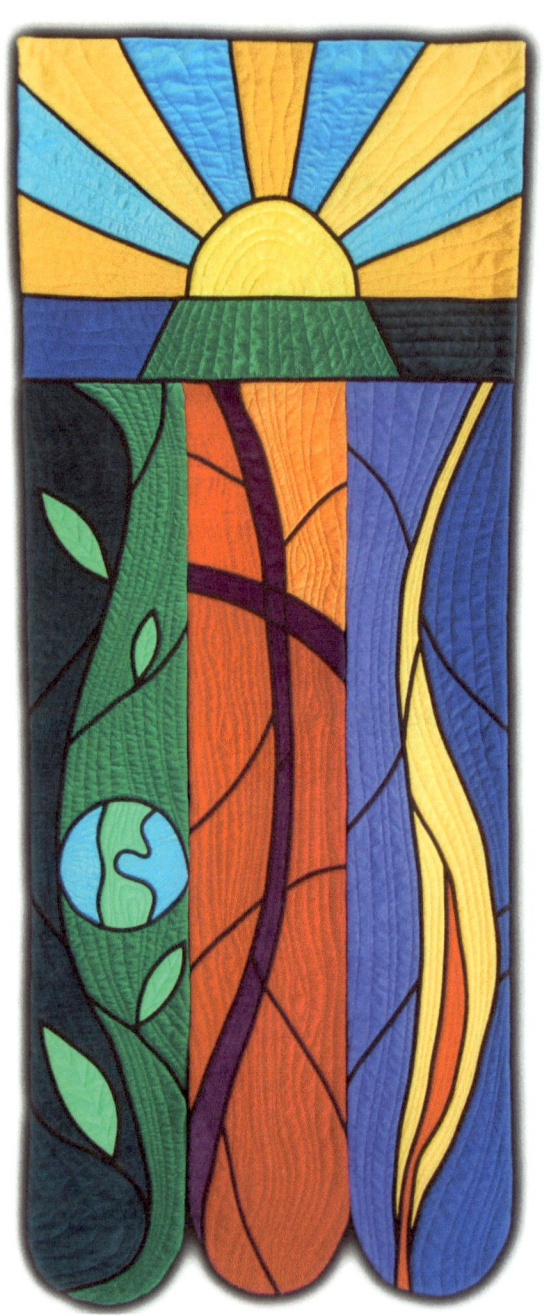

M. Bunte
West Lafayette, IN, USA

Trinity
24" x 60"

God's presence is shown to us in several ways. As Creator, He makes the beautiful, yet daunting, world in which we live. In the form of the Messiah, Jesus, He comes as an example of His love and sacrifice. The flame of His Holy Spirit encourages us to love each other and gives us hope for the future. In depicting these three aspects of God, I chose to show the light of His love spreading across the world, as symbolized by the sun, sea, and land forms. Underneath, supporting our existence, is the presence of God in the ways in which He reveals Himself.

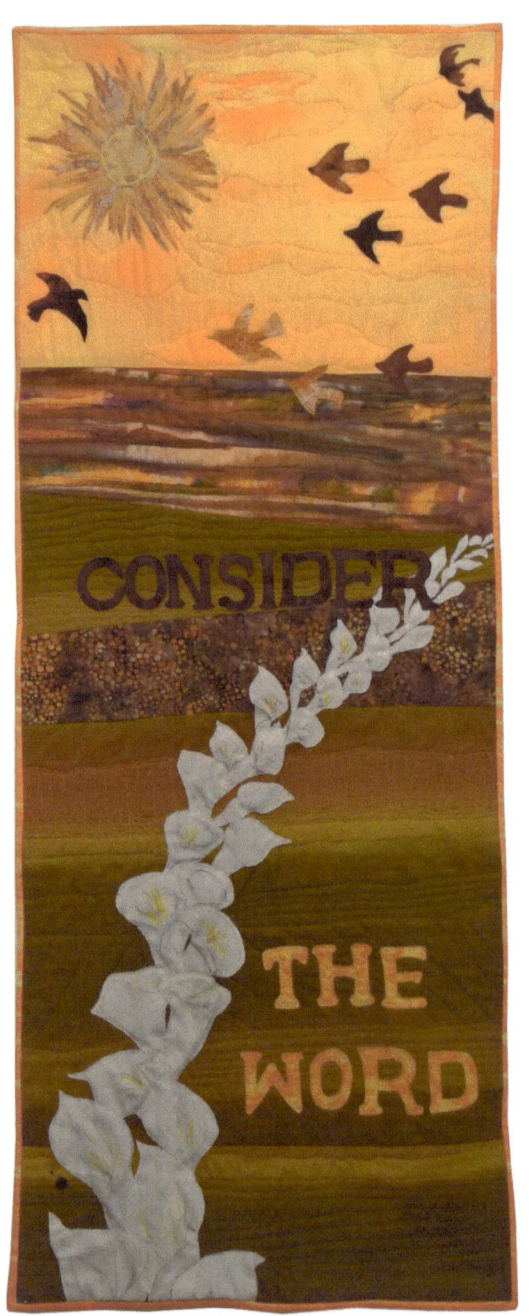

Sonia Callahan
Pledmont, CA, USA

Lilies Of The Field
24" x 60"

This quilt is about trust and belief. Both Matthew and Luke admonish us to give our worries over to God and believe that He will take care of us. God's generosity and gifts surrounds us if we open our hearts to His care. The Word asks us to consider the example of the birds of the air, which neither toil nor reap, and the beauty of lilies, regardless of the brevity of their existence.

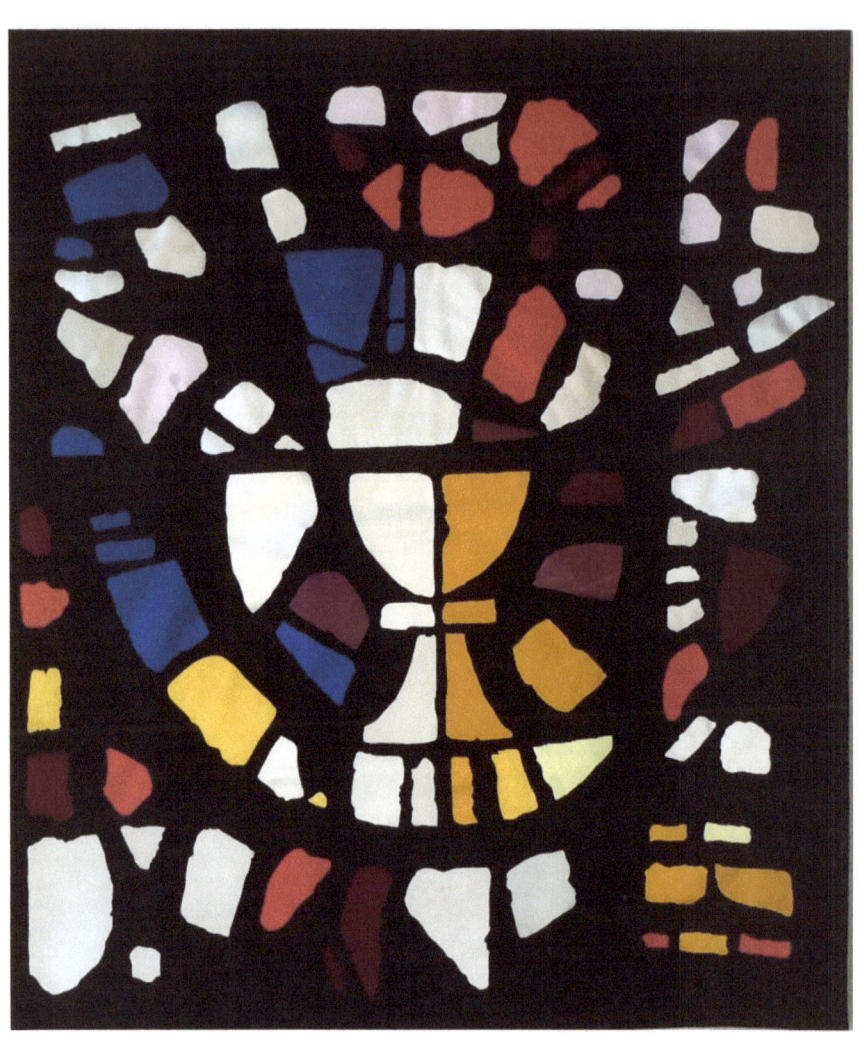

Janice Carter
San Francisco, CA, USA

Celebrate the Eucharist
33" x 39"

I made this quilt in response to a challenge issued by my local quilt guild. The subject was "Celebration." I am an Episcopalian, and am used to hearing the phrase "Celebrate the Eucharist." This seemed to be an appropriate way for me to interpret the theme of "Celebrate". In my church, Christ Episcopal Church in Los Altos, California there are beautiful stained glass windows all around the sanctuary depicting different parts of the Bible. One of my favorite windows features a chalice, which is used in the celebration of the Eucharist. My quilt is a fabric rendering of that window.

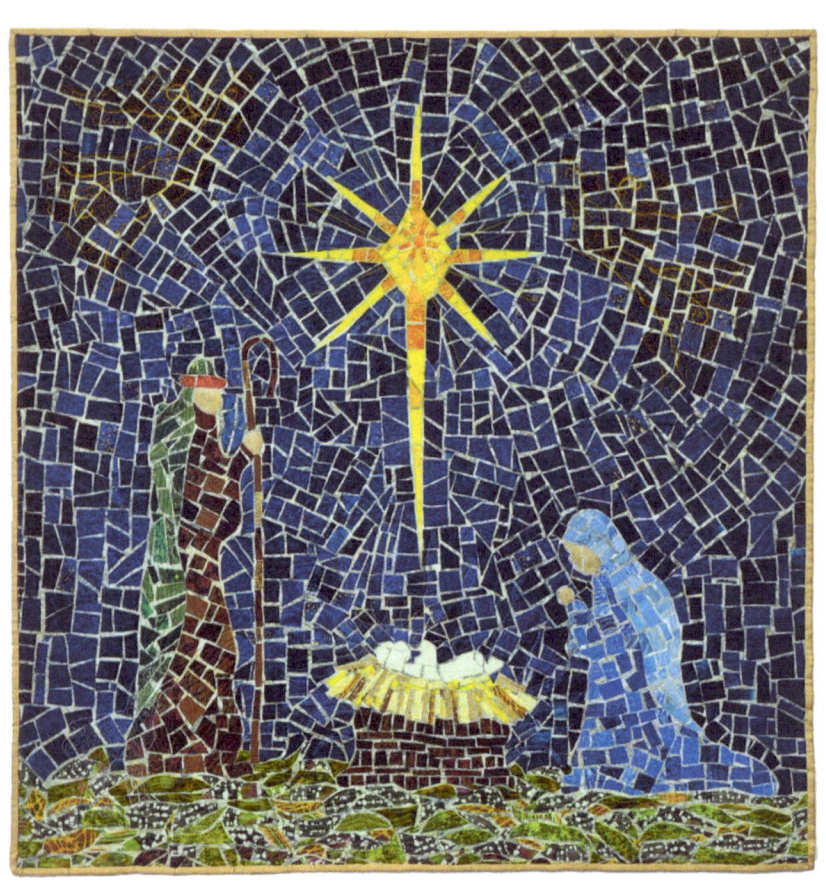

Shannon Conley
Moore, OK, USA

Rejoice, Rejoice
39" x 39"

My heart is filled with joy as the eye travels from the light of the Star of Bethlehem to the Baby Jesus.

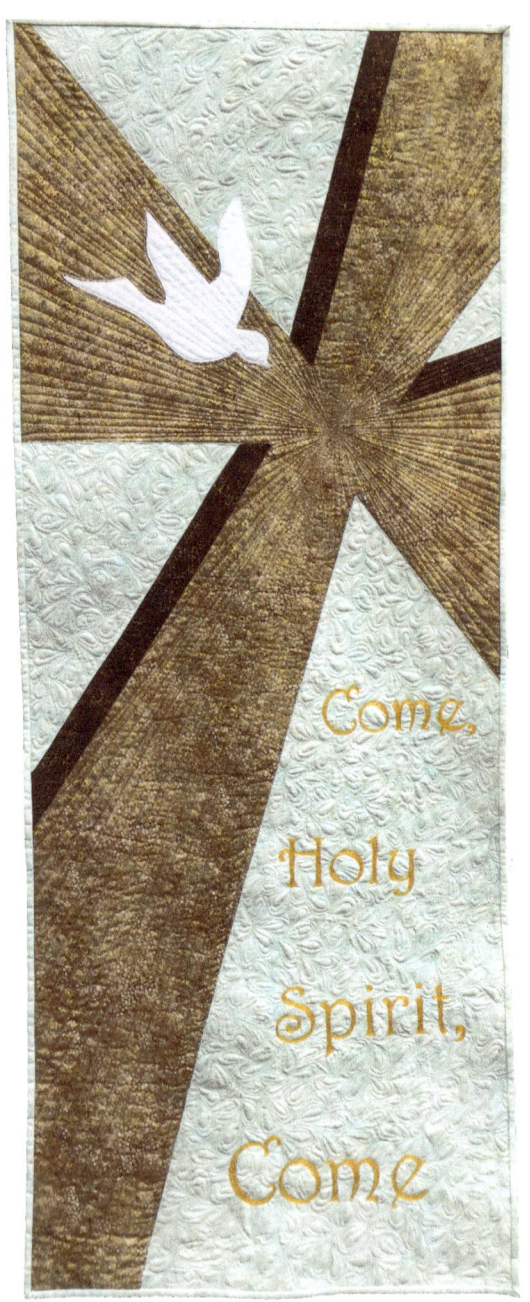

Lisa Ellis
Fairfax, VA, USA

Come, Holy Spirit, Come
24" x 60"

As we gather to worship, we call upon the Holy Spirit to fill this sacred space and lead us as we Praise His Holy Name.

"But you will receive power when the Holy Spirit comes on you; and you will be my witnesses in Jerusalem, and in all Judea and Samaria, and to the ends of the earth." Acts 1:8

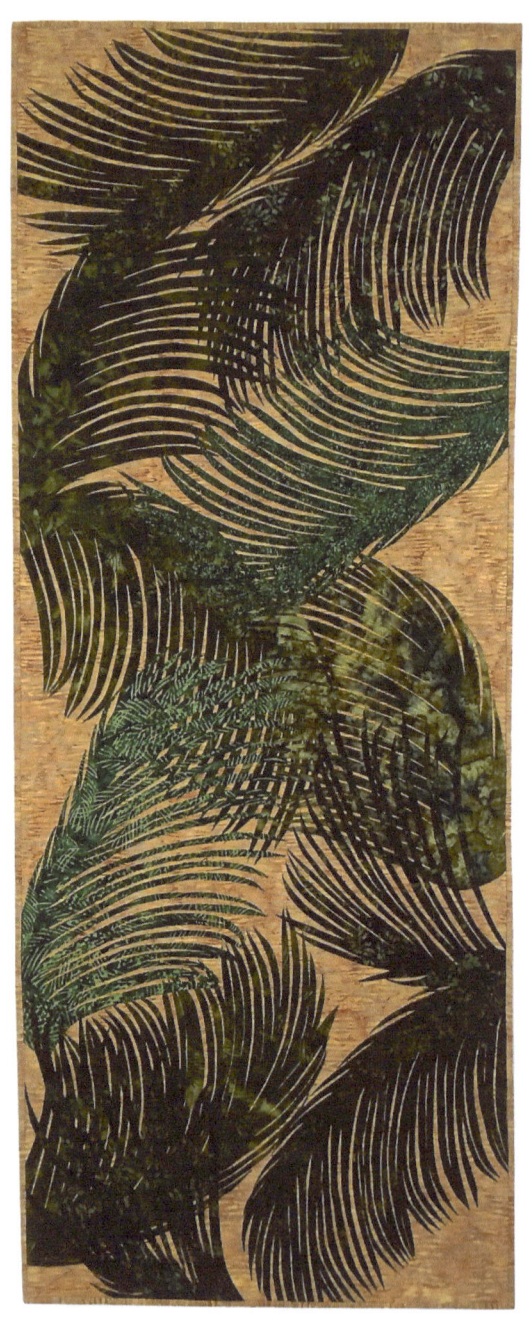

Sarah Entsminger
Ashburn, VA, USA

Road to Jerusalem
24" x 60"

The youth group at our church traditionally performs a very moving mime presentation on Palm Sunday. Listening to the music combined with the narration and acting, creates a very somber but beautiful reenactment of the scripture verses. Sitting in the pew holding my palm, I imagine what the scene might have looked like on that road to Jerusalem, as people tossed palm fronds and branches onto the path before Jesus. Those thoughts inspired me to create this quilt that illustrates those imagined palms on the road.

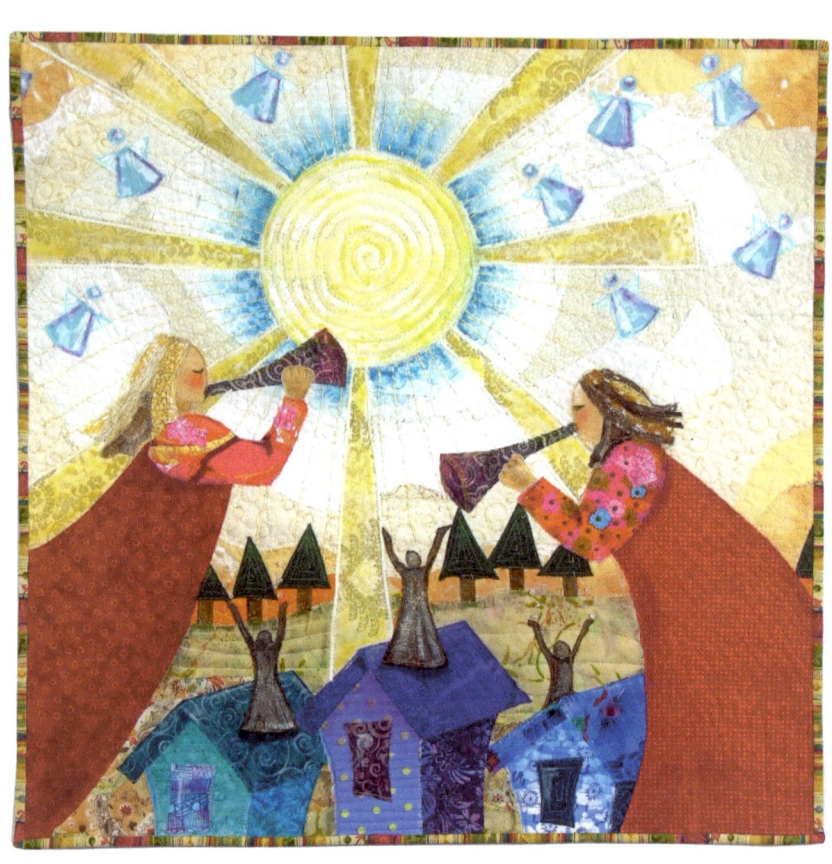

Diana Ferguson
Sweetwater, TN, USA

The Clarion Call
27" x 27"

This art quilt is an expression of the joy that we feel as humans as we are called to rejoice in our spirituality and connectivity to God. We are meant to raise up our voices in praise, thanksgiving, and love.

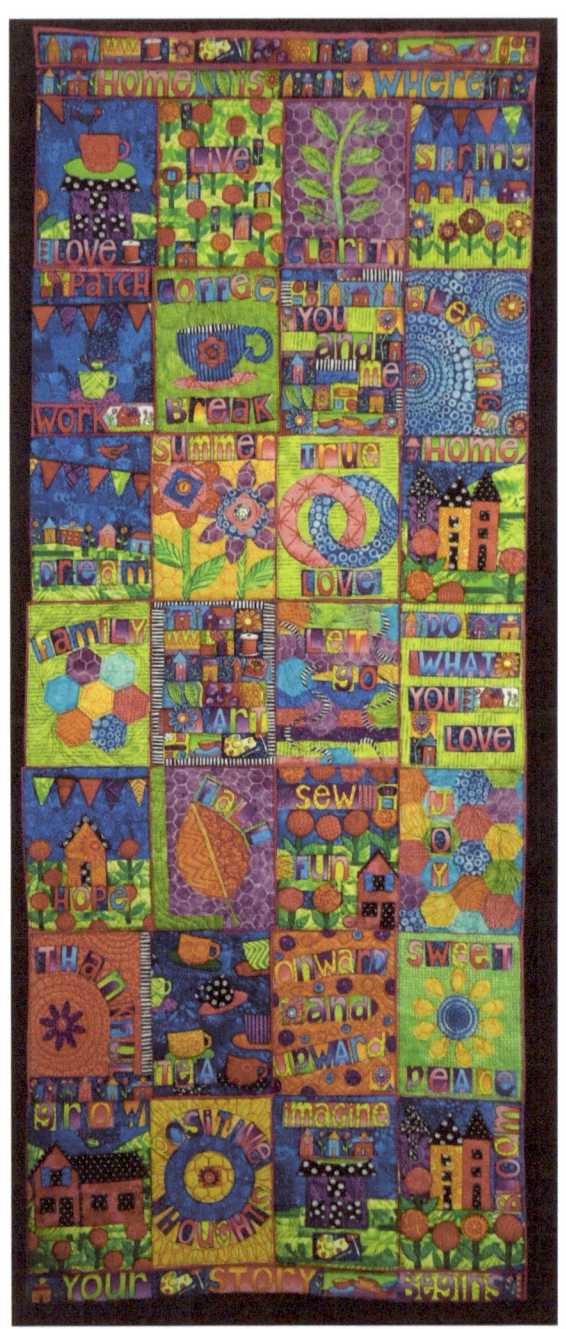

Jamie Fingal
Orange, CA, USA

Every Day Matters
24" x 60"

A collection of prayer flags inspires me to seek out the possibilities in this life, and see beyond myself. The blessings of family, friends and home . . . all that I hold dear.

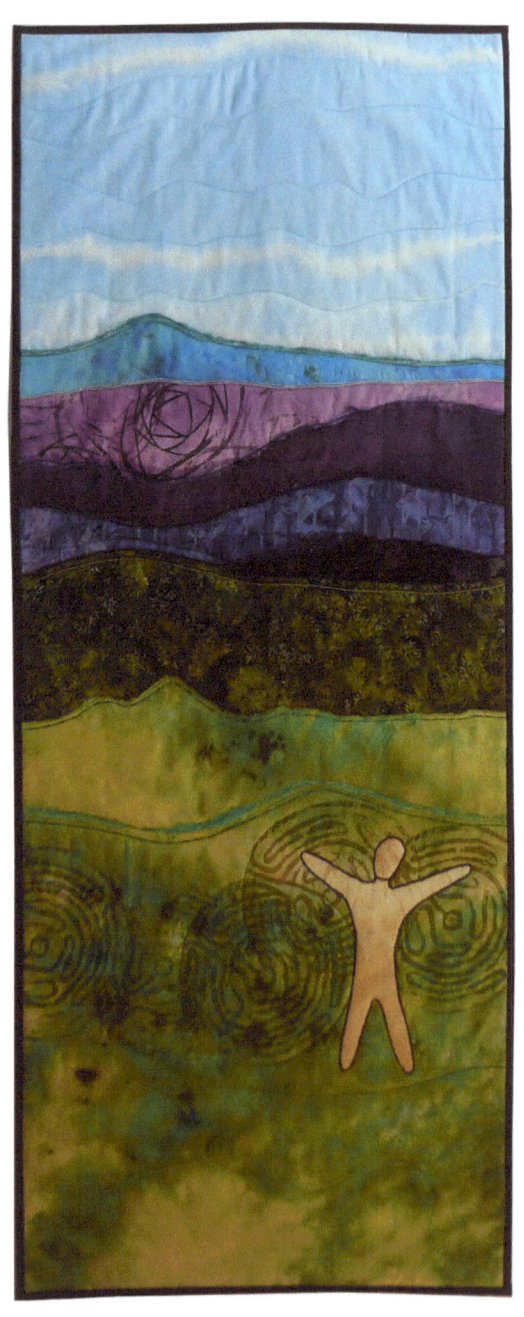

Norma Fredrickson
Berryville, VA, USA

Unto The Hills
24" x 60"

If I were a psalmist, I would look to the Blue Ridge.
Old mountains catch the mist, the snow.
Old mountains protect the valley below,
Green valley where I walk in daily patterns.

The path of the labyrinth quiets my mind
And I raise my eyes.
I lift my eyes. The hills have shadows and trees.
Goodness is there. Help is present.

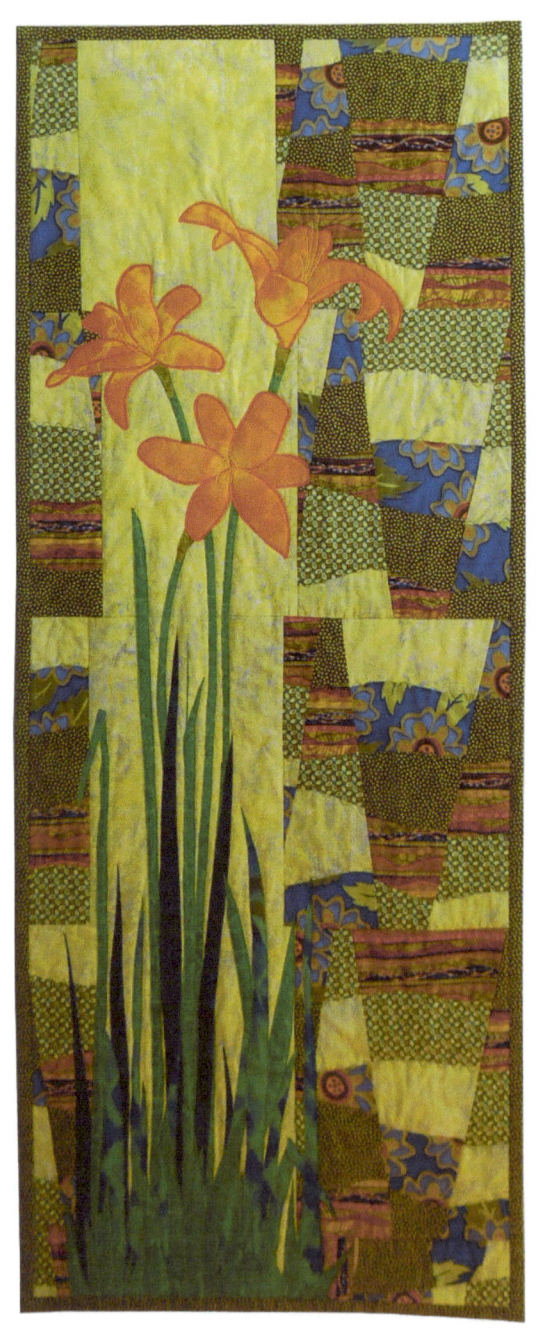

Norma Fredrickson
Berryville, VA, USA

Consider These Lilies
24" x 60"

Consider these lilies.

Growing in your very own yard. Not the ones in faraway places. Not the ones on Easter altars. Consider these lilies. The ones Mama held in disdain, but which taught you about "wabisabi" in floral arrangement. (Not that anyone near that Midwest farm knew anything about Ikebana.)

They neither sow nor reap. They bloom one day. That's it. Of course, there are plenty of buds. Blossoms appear abundantly for many summer days. These one day bloomers persevere, returning each spring after deep cold, deep snow. Could I be of their stock? I will consider these lilies.

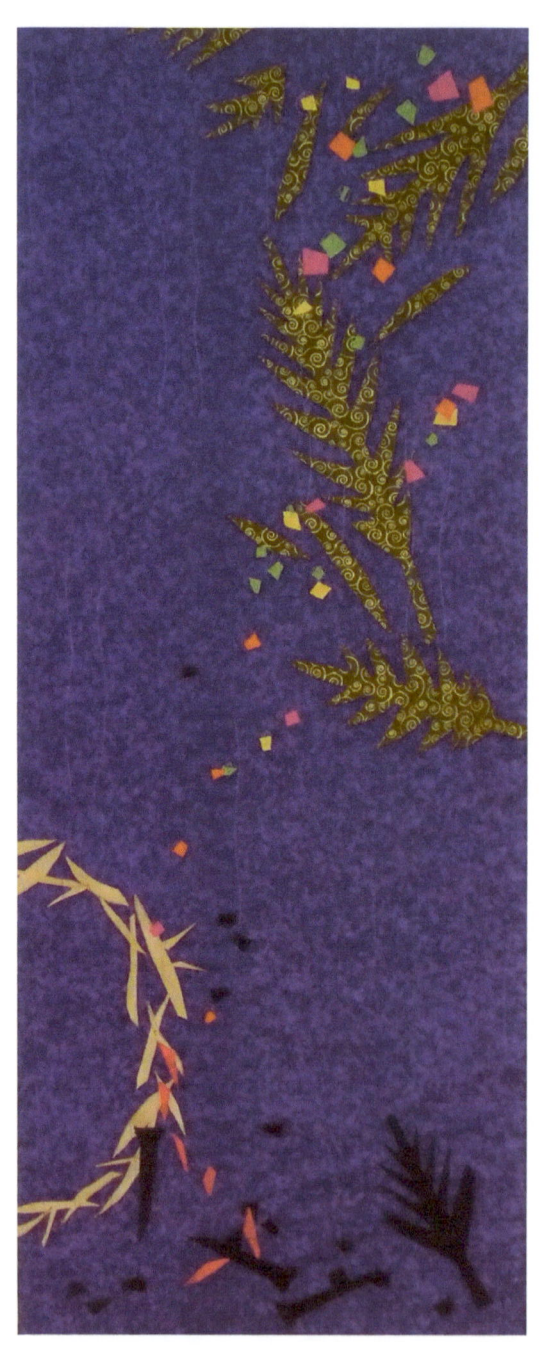

Jenny Gallo
White Lake, MI, USA

Holy Week Journey
24" x 60"

This banner reflects the story we remember during Holy Week. The palm parade, crown of thorns and nails are enhanced by the texture of fabric confetti. Placed as if the parade had just passed by, it is at first joyful and then turns to the impending darkness. The shape of the palm leaves mimic a spear shape and therefore the banner is completed with a palm in black to recall Jesus' side being pierced. Like our sin mocks God's love for us the purple background recalls the cloak that was mockingly placed on Jesus.

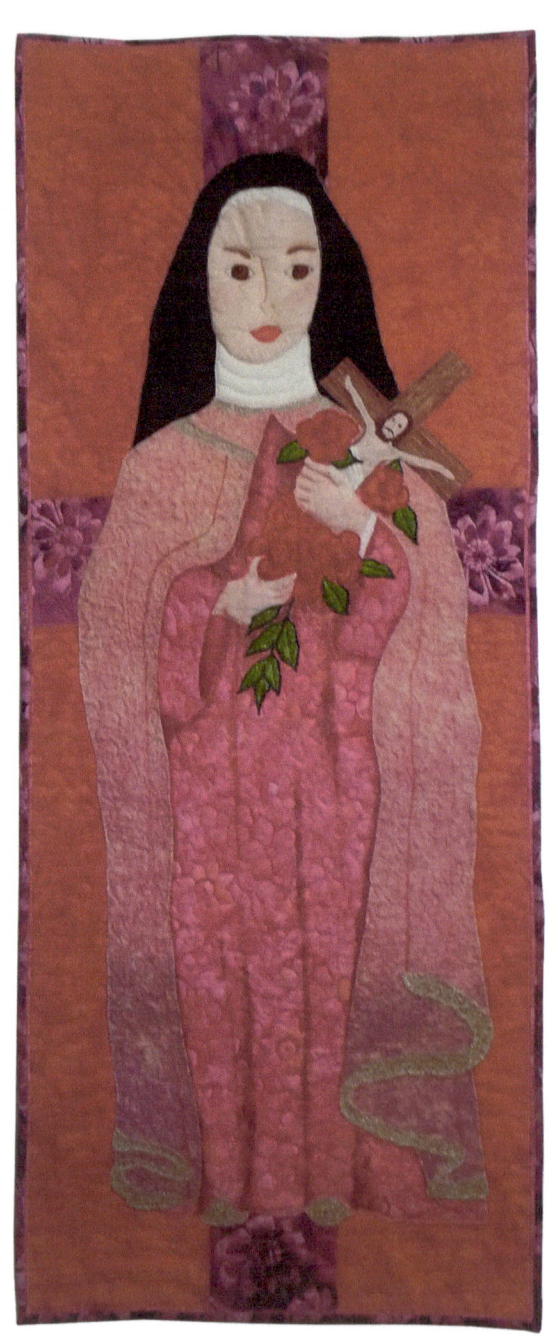

Laura Gilmartin
Stafford, VA, USA

St. Theresa
24" x 60"

St. Theresa is my Mom's patron saint. While visiting friends in New Mexico I fell in love with the primitive images of religious figures. I saw a fabric that I fell in love with that had several religious images. My quilt represents one of the Saints on the fabric. My Mom continues to inspire me even though she is no longer with me.

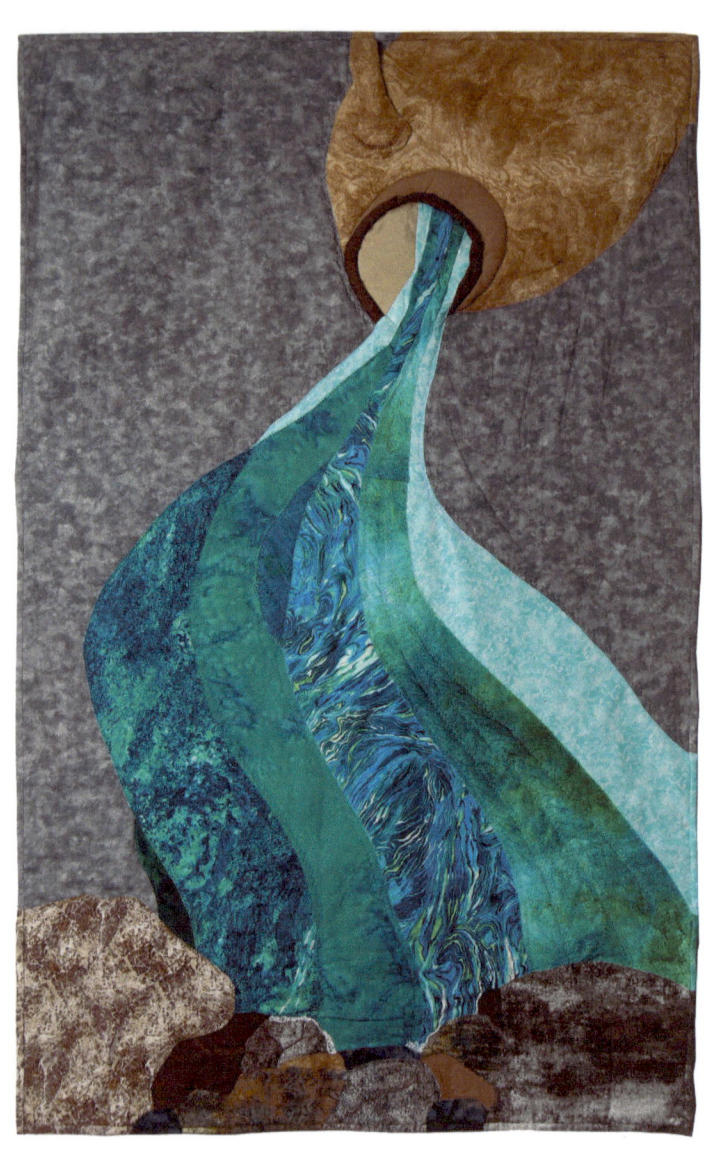

Linda Hall
Gahanna, OH, USA

Poured Out
36" x 60"

A procession of colorful banners, reflecting a personal statement of faith and service, preceded each candidate for ordination. "Poured Out" was designed for Nicole Baker, Associate Pastor of Stonybrook Methodist Church in Gahanna, Ohio. The verses that anchor Nikki's life and ministry are from Philippians 2:5-11. This is referred to as the Kenosis Hymn. "Kenosis", Greek for "emptying out", reflects Christ's humility as He came to serve not be served. This represents Nikki's ministry, working alongside the people of Stonybrook. The pouring water draws us to remember our baptism. The stones represent Stonybrook as the water mingles around the rocks.

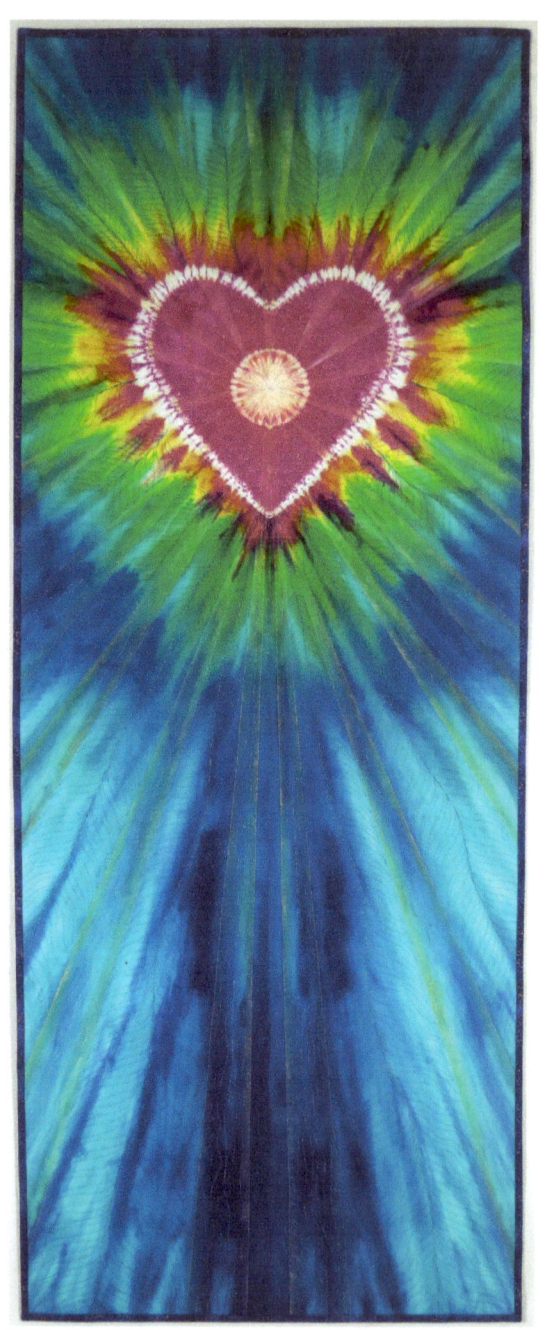

Ginnie Hebert
Puyallup, WA, USA

Open Heart
24" x 60"

Recently I tie-dyed hearts with a class of second graders. The 24 hearts were then sewn into a quilt to be auctioned at a fundraiser. I was so inspired by the quilt's beauty that I resolved to make an art piece using a shibori heart. The heart is a universal symbol of love; an open heart a representation of releasing the spirit of God from within. What better image for a sacred space?

"The most valuable possession you can own is an open heart. The most powerful weapon you can be is an instrument of peace." Carlos Santana

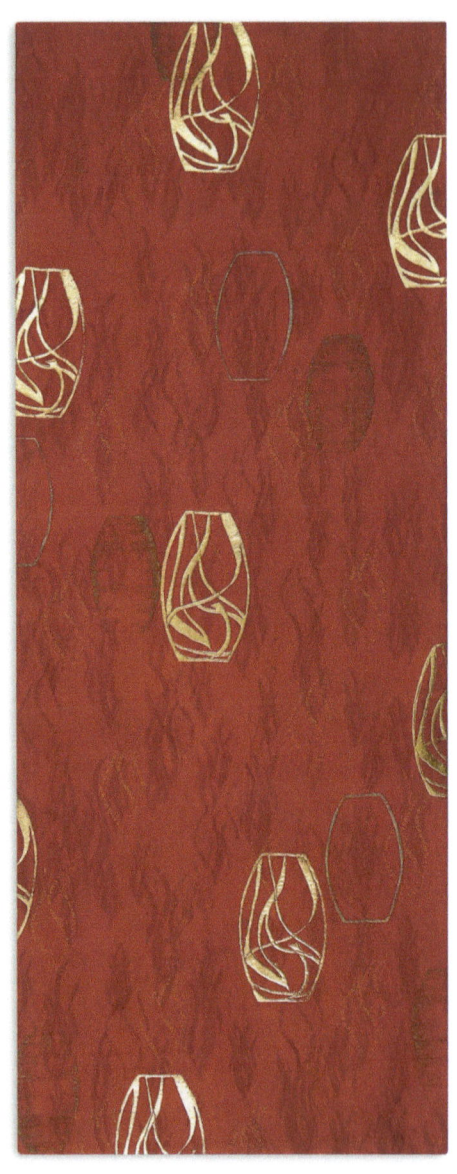

Linda Henke
Indianapolis, IN, USA

Vessel: Spirit-Filled
24" x 60"

For the past twelve years, I have worked as a full-time studio artist, creating commissioned projects for churches of various denominations and sizes, denominational headquarters, religious agencies, and individuals around the globe.

As the design process for each project unfolds, I come to heightened awareness that the creative impulse does not flow from me but rather through me. This awareness, which provided inspiration for "Vessel: Spirit-Filled", finds expression in images of primitive vessels, abstracted flames/doves, artfully configured text [Exodus 31.3], and the vibrant, unrestrained liturgical color of Pentecost.

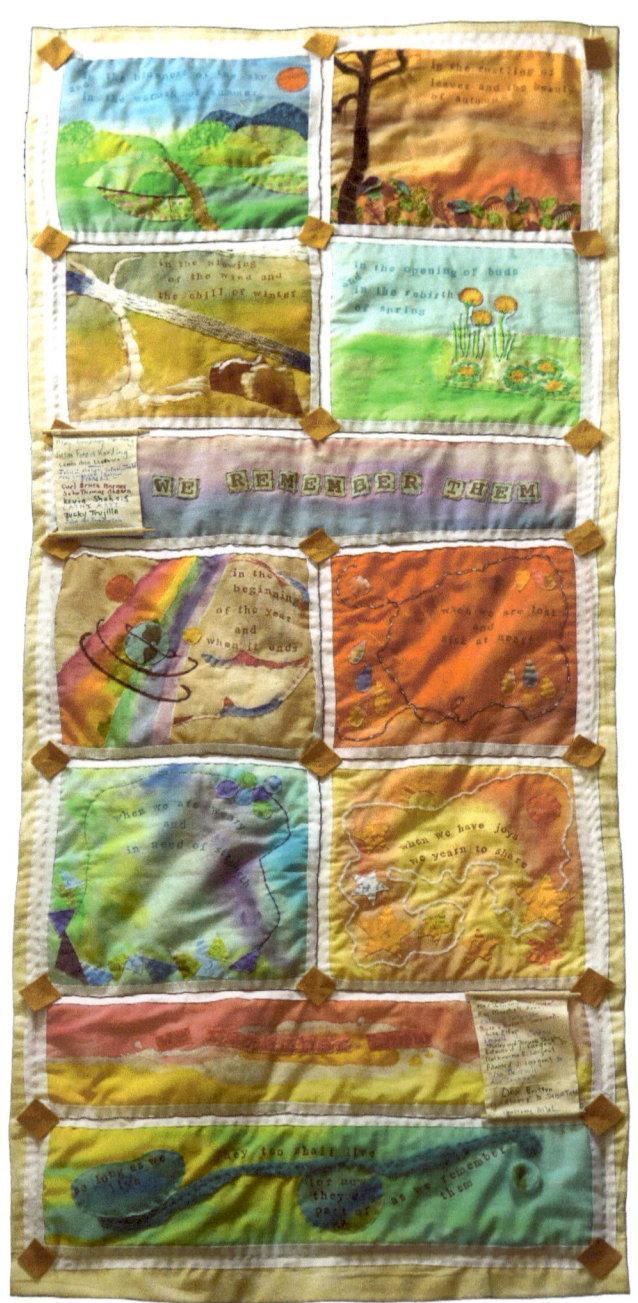

Etta Johnson
Vienna, VA, USA

We Remember Them
25" x 58"

Depicting the nine verses of the ancient Jewish "we remember them" prayer in fabric graphics helped me to express the grief of my husband's death. From crafting the first panel - "In the rising of the sun, and in its going down" to the last – "so long as they live, we too shall live," I discovered that creating beauty reduces pain. In addition, friend and family members had a concrete way to remember their lost loved ones by writing their names on a scroll on the hanging. "We Remember Them" combines fabric painting, appliqué, and quilting.

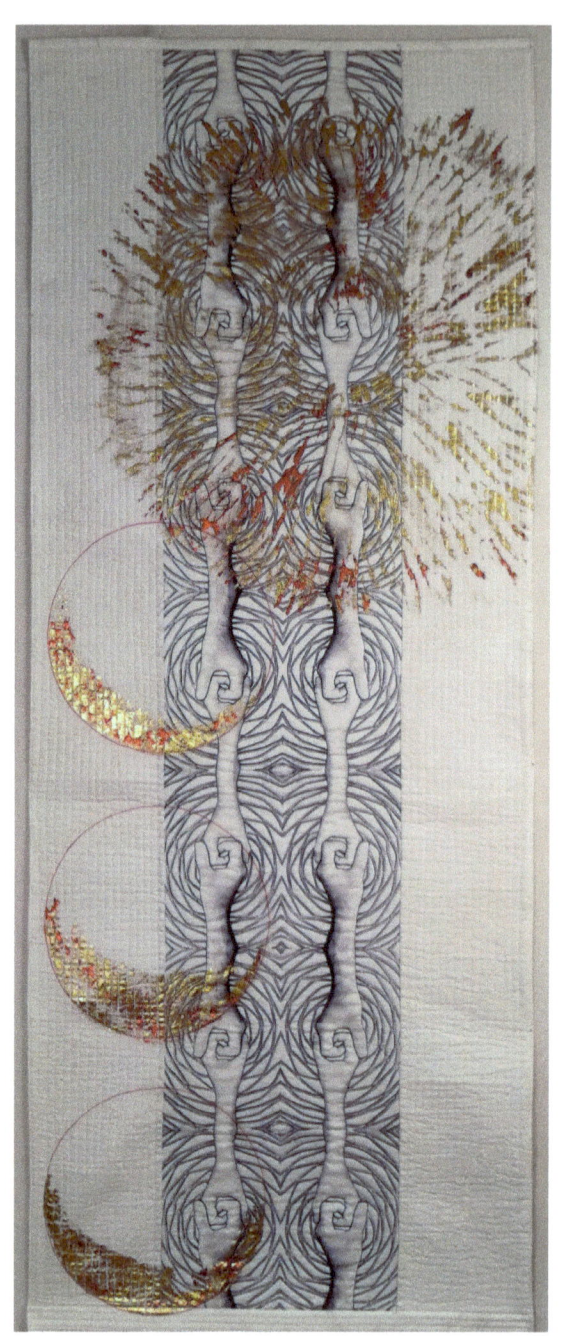

Lyric Kinard
Cary, NC, USA

Linked
24" x 60"

Our time on earth is to be used compassionately, to forge connections between families and generations, between ourselves and our God, between individuals and all of humanity. Each individual is a link in an eternal chain.

The photograph of the artist and her husband's linked hands was taken by Julia Wade and used by permission.

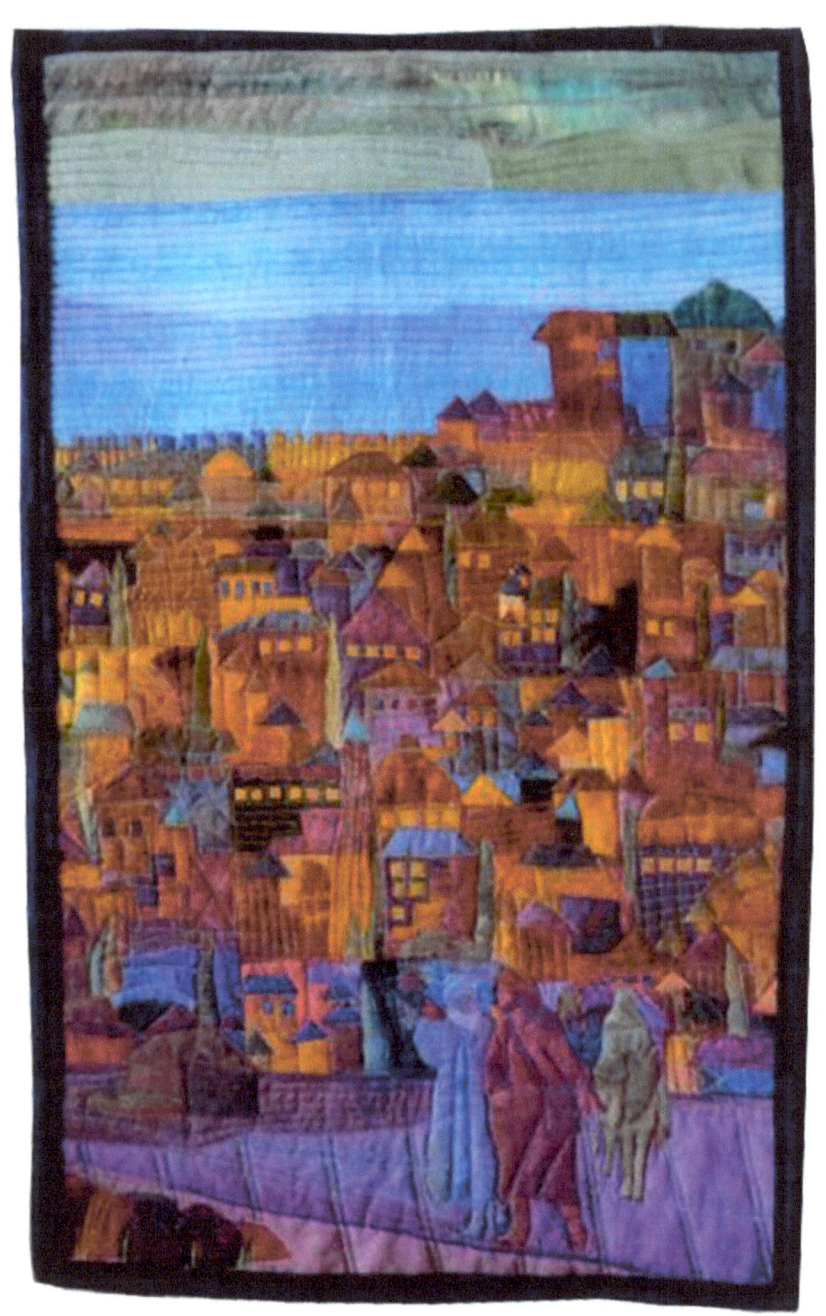

Janice Neisius
Canon City, CO, USA

No Room At The Inn
21" x 32.5"

A pilgrimage to Bethlehem and Jerusalem, visiting all the sacred places, was the inspiration for this quilt. I saw the star placed on the floor in the Church of the Nativity where the stable existed and Christ was born. I embellished the quilt in twilight colors to show how weary Mary and Joseph were in finding no room at the inn.

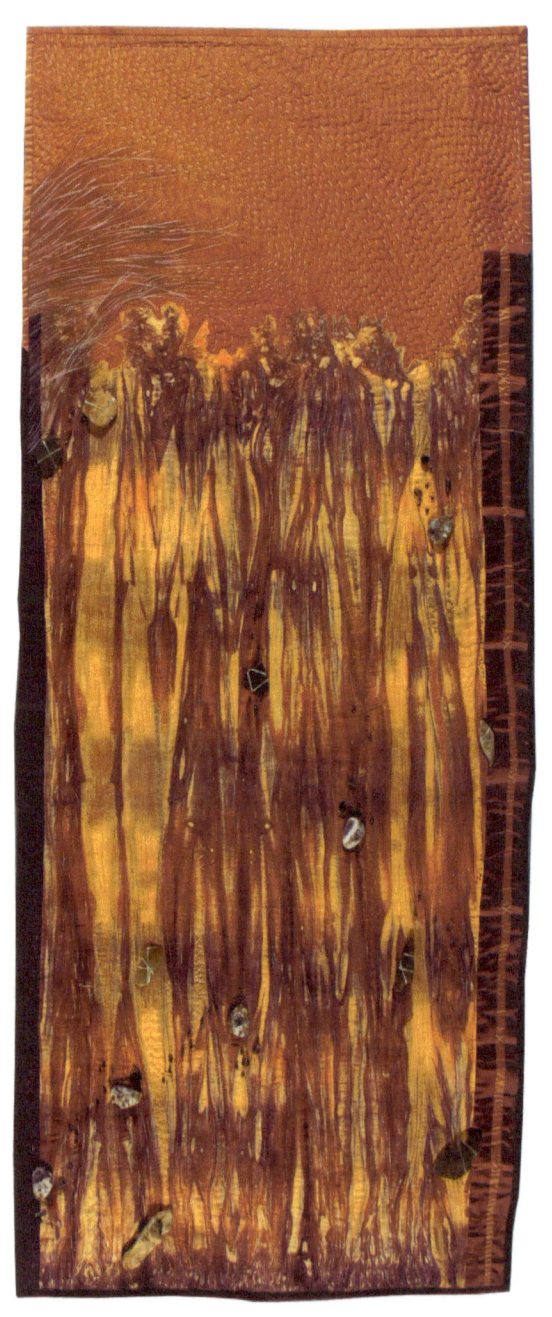

Bobbe Shapiro Nolan
Eagle Lake, TX, USA

Out Into the Wilderness
24” x 60”

"And the Spirit immediately drove him out into the wilderness. He was in the wilderness forty days, tempted by Satan; and he was with the wild beasts; and the angels waited on him." Mark 1:12-13

Wilderness can be many things: refuge, threat, challenge, peace, solitude, beauty, loneliness, thirst, heat, cold, memory, emptiness, waiting, and more. It is there when we need it, whether we know it or not. Sometimes we run toward, or from, wilderness; sometimes we're driven.

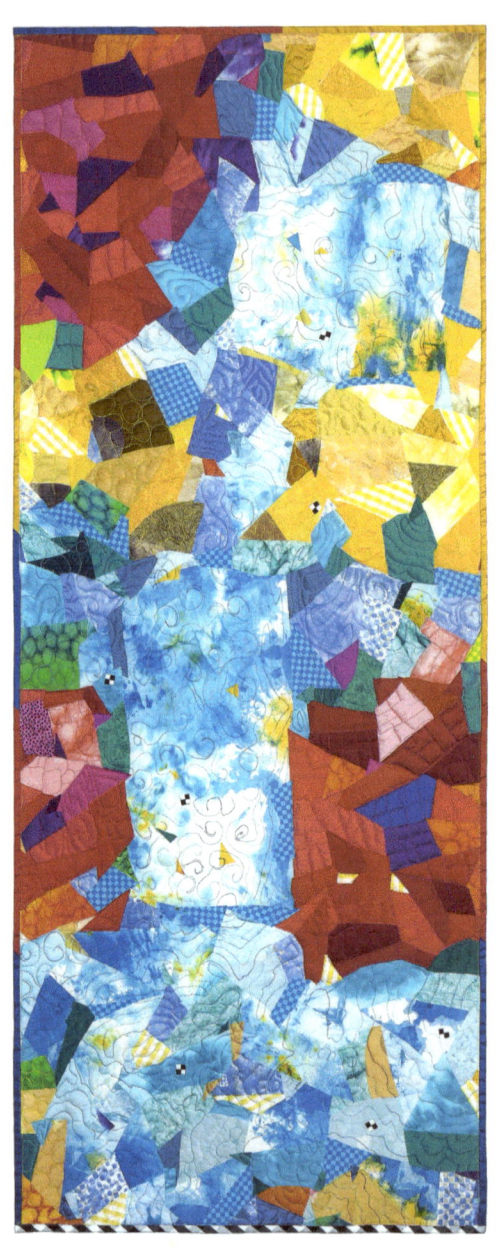

Yvonne Porcella
Modesto, CA, USA

Primarily Water
24" x 60"

Water and the Word, two elements pertinent to our faith and essential to life. Without spiritual water and free flowing water the world and the people in it would not survive. The addition of red and gold emphasizes the alternative to lack of water – dry earth and fire.

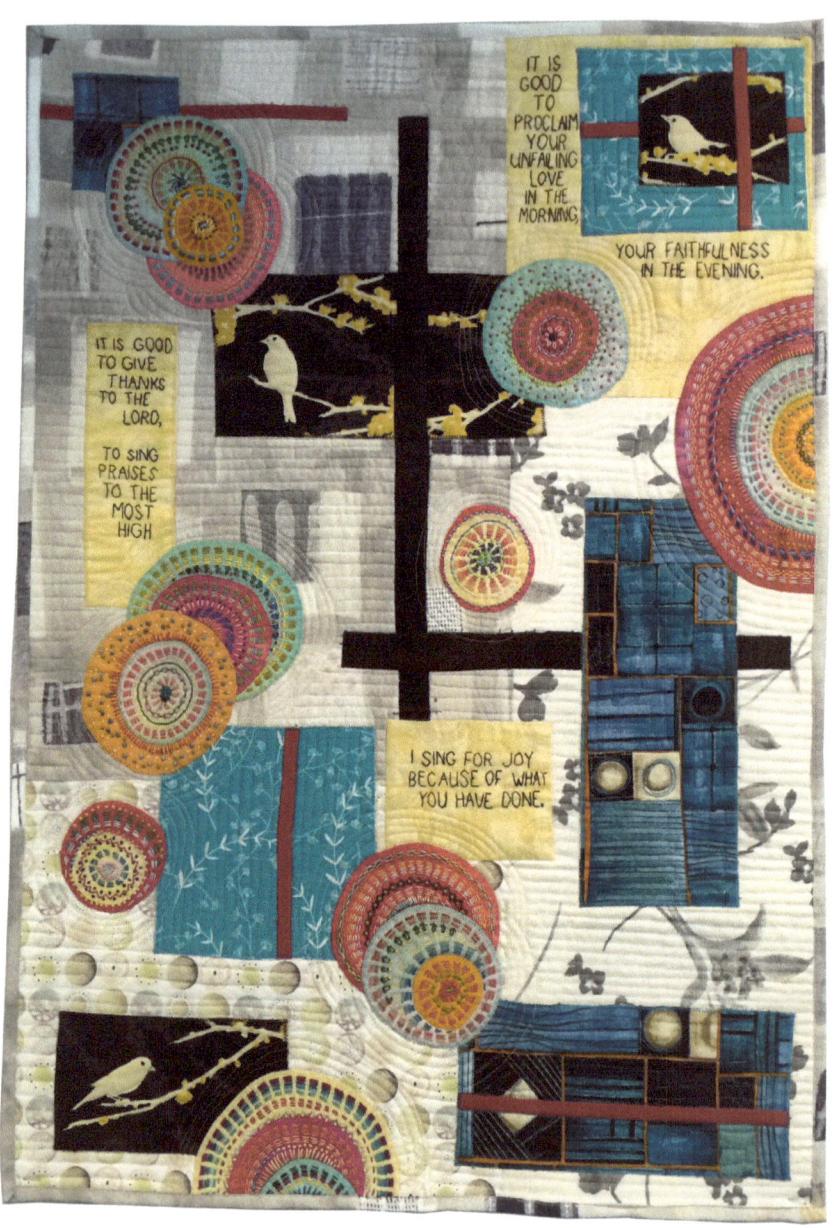

Debby Schnabel
Pine Grove, CA, USA

Sing for Joy
23" x 33"

As the birds became a central image on this quilt, I knew I had to find a psalm that would include singing and the joy that it brings.

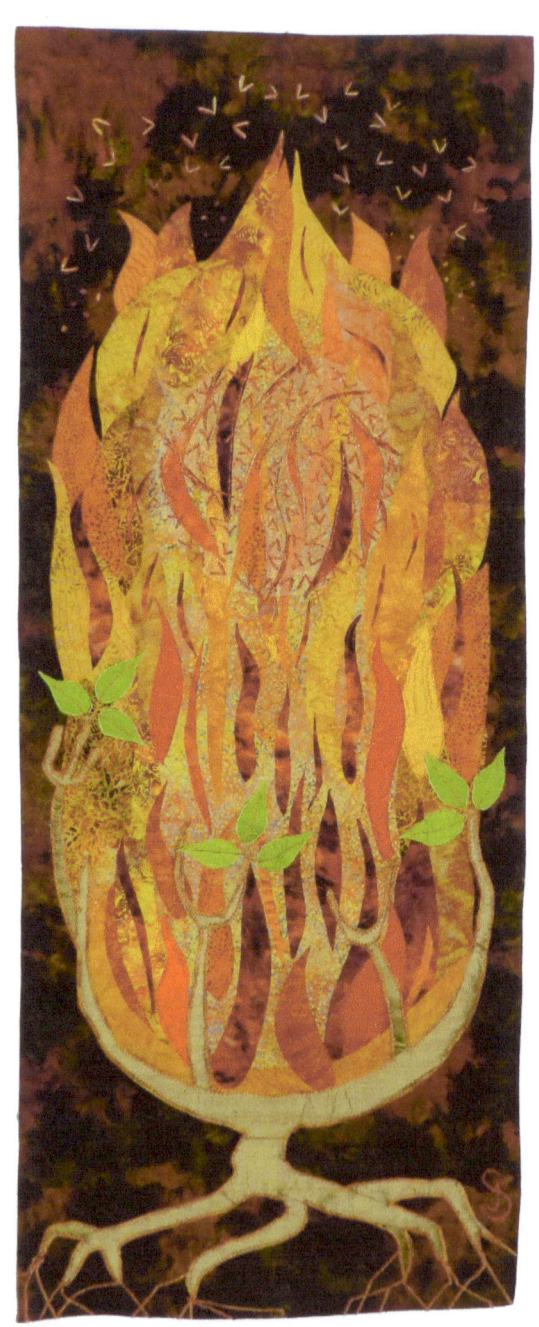

Joan Stogis
Silver Spring, MD, USA

Burning Bush
24" x 60"

The Burning Bush is firmly rooted in ordinary earth, but has divine fire within it. Although the fire rages, three live branches are in leaf, each with three green leaves – a hint of the future triune definition of God. High in the column of flame, hand embroidered "sparks" convey the intense energy of Yahweh who speaks to Moses – and to all who are called.

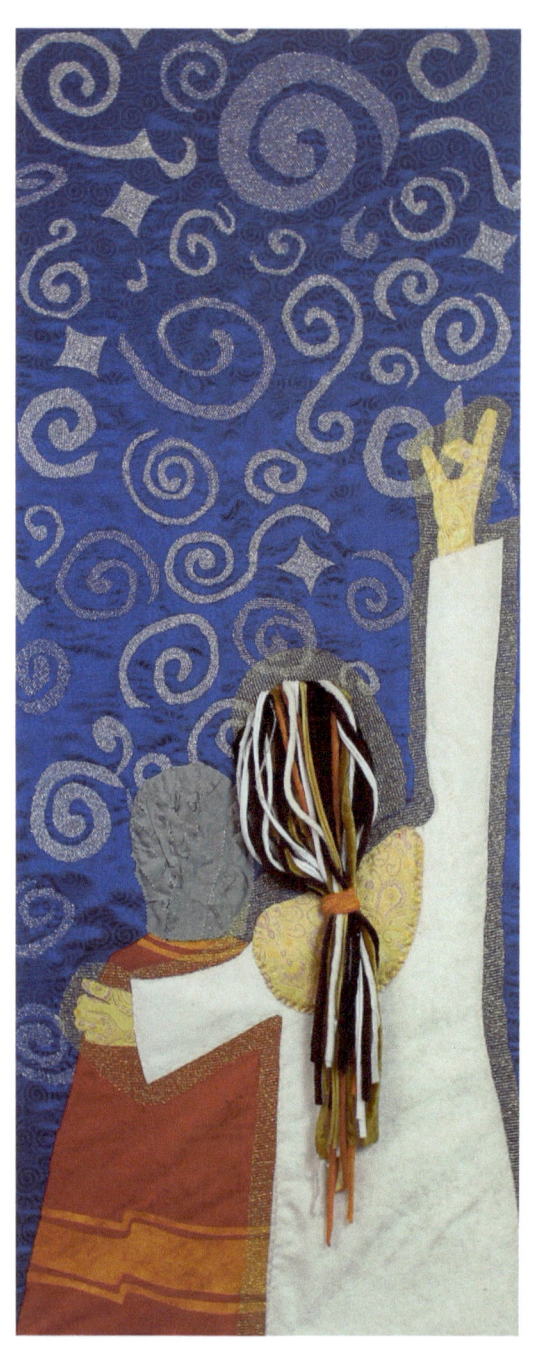

Suzanne Thompson
Sainte Genevieve, MO, USA

Abraham, God, and a Starry Night
24" x 60"

Several years ago I was taking a course in the Old Testament when I realized that Christianity, Islam, and Judaism share a common ancestor, Abraham. I chose to illustrate a story in this piece about Abraham that represents his close relationship with God, never hesitating to express doubt or disagreement. It comes down to faith.

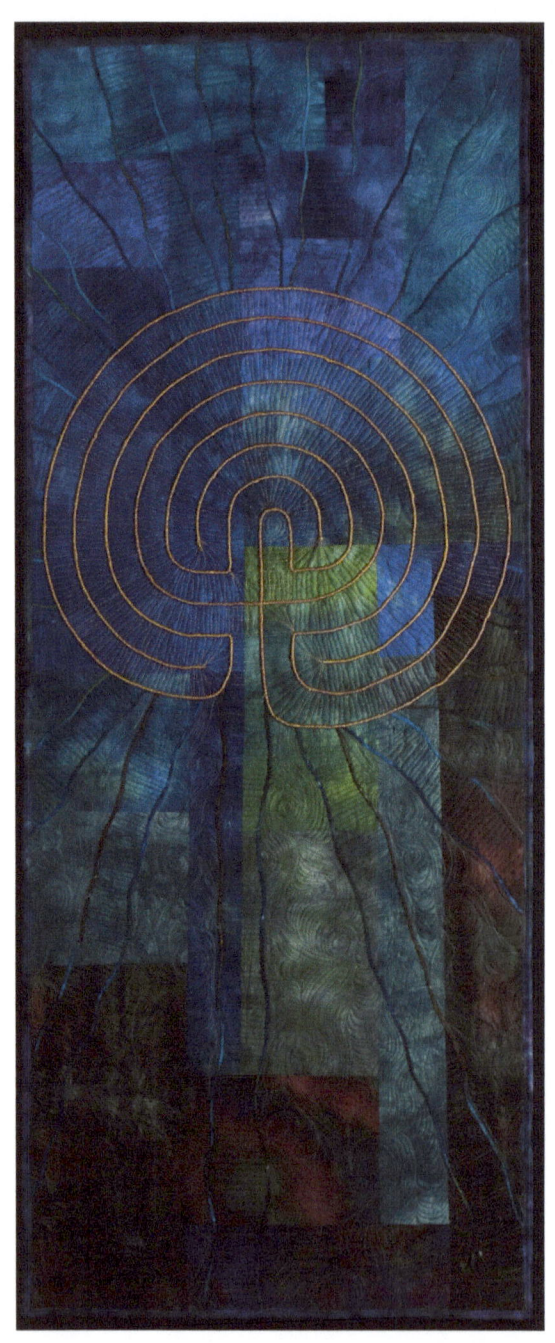

Larkin Van Horn
Freeland, WA, USA

Solvitur Ambulando
24" x 60"

The title, attributed to St. Augustine, translates to: "It is solved by walking". The labyrinth was, and is, a common form of walking meditation, appearing in ancient stone carvings and the floor of Chartres Cathedral in France, among others. Today, labyrinths are designed for fields, floors, fingertips, and painted on cloths that can be rolled up and stored when not in use.

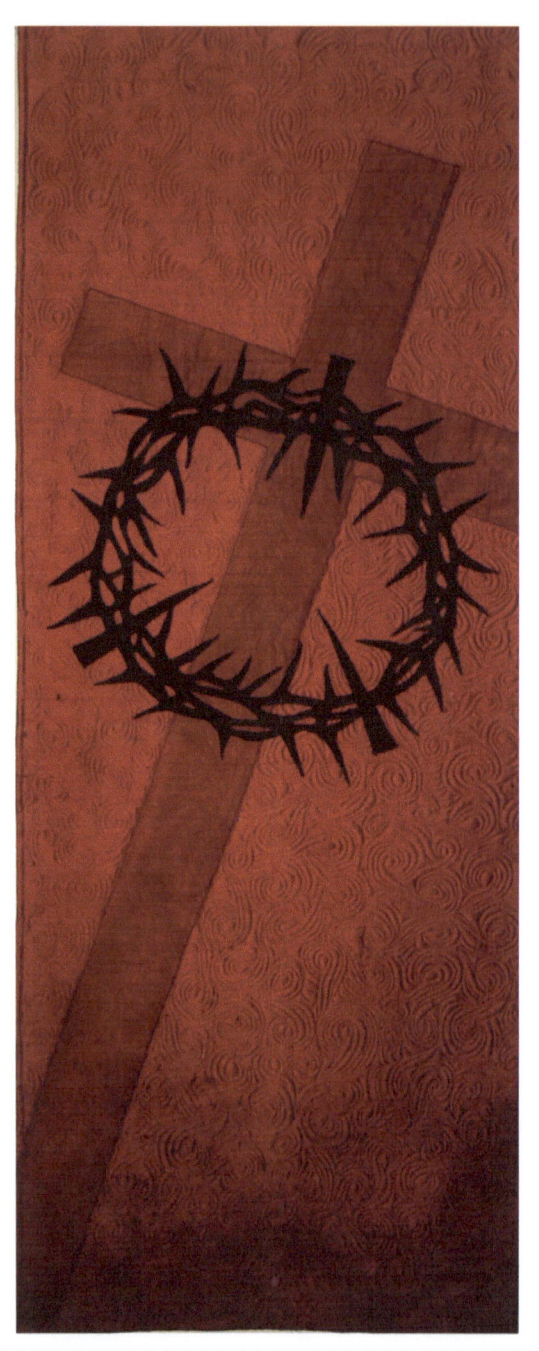

Traci Warnke
Lisbon, WI, USA

Crown of Thorns
24" x 60"

The pain and suffering of Jesus Christ and His sacrifice for us.

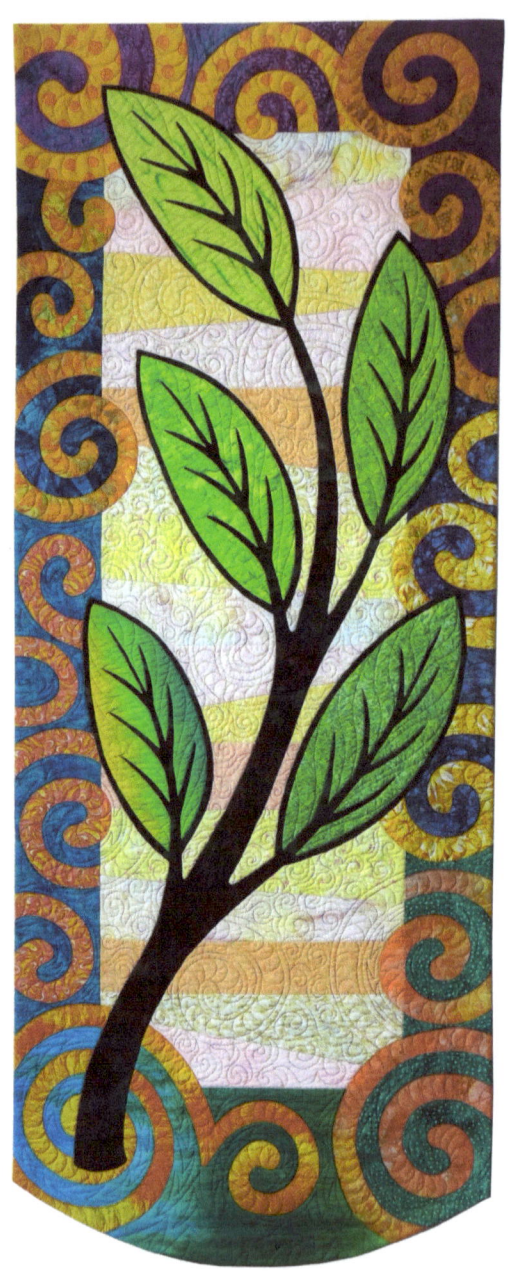

Rachel Wetzler
St. Charles, IL, USA

New Life
24" x 60"

"Because of his great mercy he gave us new life by raising Jesus Christ from death. This fills us with a living hope." (I Peter 1:3)

"In God's Kingdom humans are rescued in order to take their place not only as receivers of forgiveness and new life but also as agents of it . . . What we're here for is to become genuine human beings reflecting the God in whose image we're made . . . The way this works out is that it produces, through the work of the Holy Spirit, a transformation of character." (After You Believe by N. T. Wright)

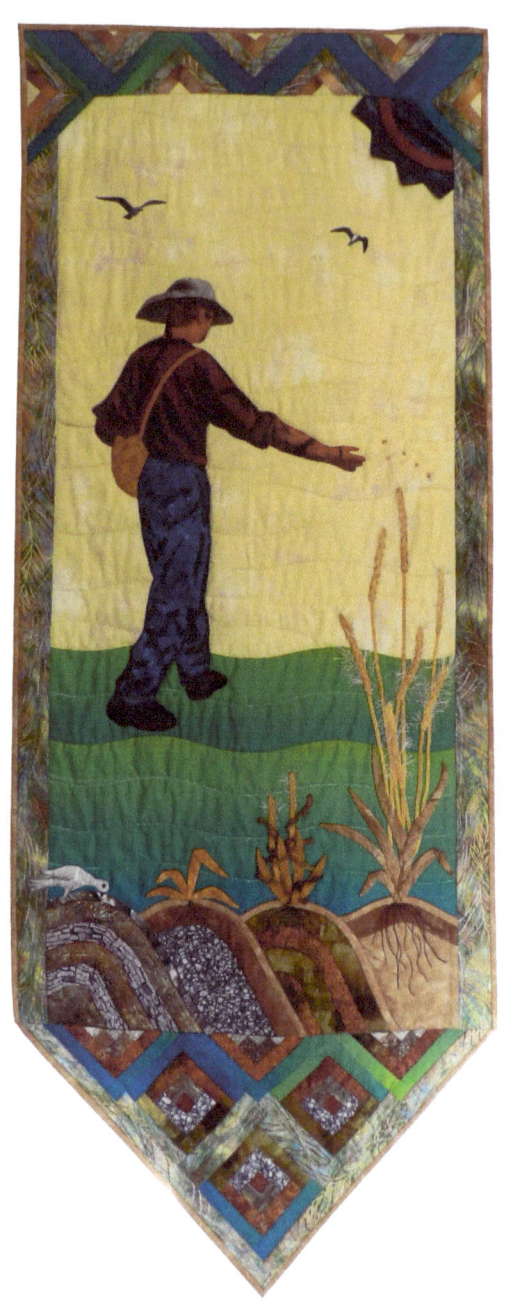

Rosanne Williamson
Warrenton, VA, USA

The Sower
24" x 60"

Inspired by illumination and scripture from The Saint John's Bible, "The Sower" shows the familiar parable told by Jesus. The seeds represent the Word of God, some falling on the path to be eaten by birds, others on the rocky ground to wither and die. Sometimes the message is choked by the thorns of the world – greed and selfishness. But some seeds fall on good soil where they grow to produce fruit, feeding the world. "Let anyone with ears to hear, listen."

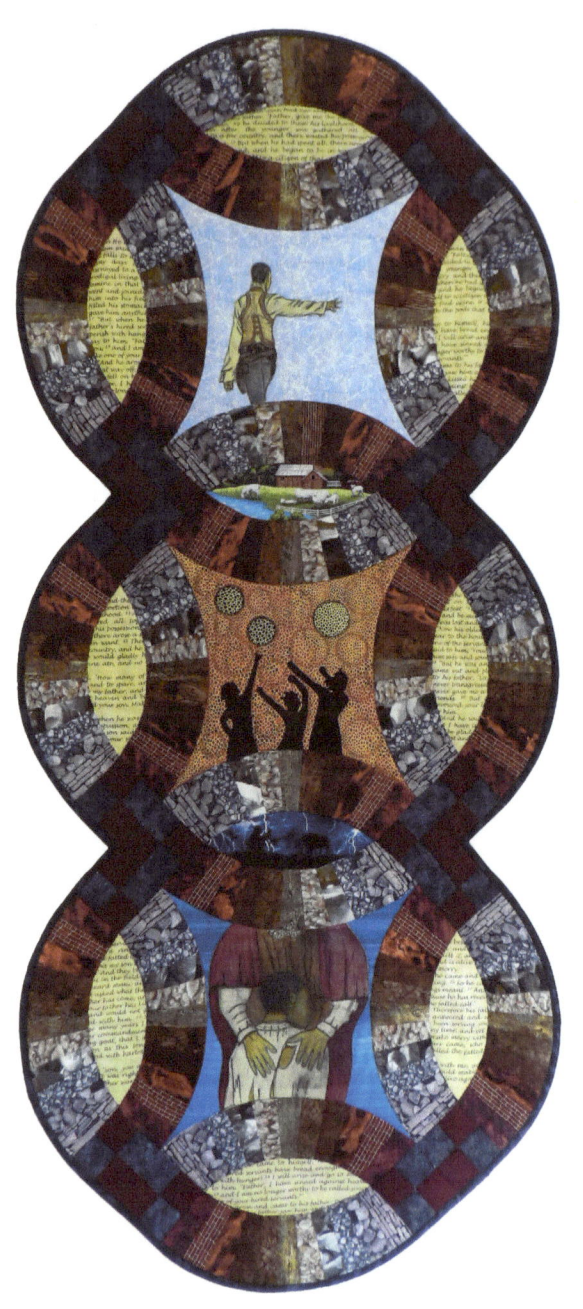

Rosanne Williamson
Warrenton, VA, USA

The Prodigal Son
24" x 54"

Jesus' beautiful story of the forgiving father is set in the traditional double wedding ring circles to show family connections and pieced to show the many paths a wayward child may travel. The young man throws his past away as he leaves home. After wild parties and false friends, the money is gone. "When he comes to himself", he goes home and is welcomed by his loving father. What comfort to know that our Heavenly Father does the same for his children!

(Father and son image inspired by Rembrandt's Prodigal Son)

Index